To Kathleen

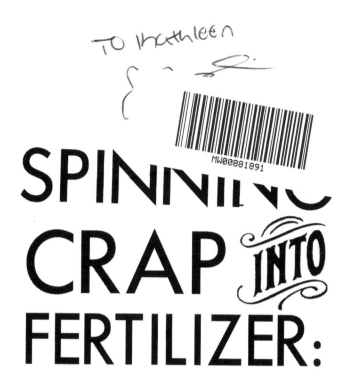

SPINNING
CRAP INTO
FERTILIZER:

How American Christianity Has
Forgotten the Necessity of Suffering

sarahbeth caplin

Copyright © 2019 by Sarahbeth Caplin
First Paperback Edition: August 2019
Cover image from DreamsTime
Cover design by Amy Queau

Library of Congress Cataloging-in-Publication Data

Caplin, Sarahbeth
Spinning Crap Into Fertilizer: How American Christianity Has Forgotten the Necessity of Suffering — 1st edition

For my frog's ribbit, duck's quack, and cow's moo.
You know who you are.

Table of Contents

HOW LONG, O LORD?
WILL YOU FORGET ME FOREVER?
HOW LONG WILL YOU HIDE YOUR
FACE FROM ME?

Psalm 13:1

Foreword

There's a verse in Scripture that bothers me. If I'm being honest, there are several troubling verses but I have learned that's the gift of the Bible. It invites us to know God intimately and to wrestle with him even in the difficult passages, demanding a blessing. What a great privilege, what a gift of grace, that we can wrestle with the creator of everything.

> *"And the Lord restored the fortunes of Job*
> *when he had prayed for his friends;*
> *and the Lord gave Job twice as much as he had before."*

Job 42:10 (NRSV)

But.

Job still suffered tremendously. His heart and his body bore scars. He lost everything dear to him. Logic doesn't explain suffering, especially when you're in the throes of it. Common phrases and well-intentioned Bible verses often do nothing but suck the air out of the room.

The answer to "why" may never come.

I have suffered. In my early-30s, I stood beside the casket of my deceased father. There were more questions than answers. One by one, friends and family from my hometown, the people who know me best, stood before me. I remember very few words spoken. I remember instead the hugs, the tears, the presence of loved ones. I felt held, lifted up by a common grief for the man we'd all lost. I also remember the comfort I experienced every time I took a Bible in my hand and read the Psalms for weeks following the funeral.

Sarahbeth tackles a topic in this book that everyone faces—suffering. We don't make our way through life without it. Suffering take the form of everyday burdens like financial strain and ongoing health concerns to events of a more catastrophic variety like tragic death and violence of global proportions. Sarahbeth tells her readers, The Christian view of suffering, in a nutshell, is that it can bring us closer to Christ, even if 'closer' means going straight to heaven and bypassing the rest of our lives on earth. It means we do not suffer alone, whether we are taken or left to survive another few decades. In either scenario, there is no easy peace."

No easy peace. When suffering shows up at our door, we wrestle for the blessing. Here are the blessings I have found in suffering:

We enter into the suffering of Jesus. Our great intercessor knows what it's like to suffer here on this earth. You don't suffer alone.

The Holy Spirit leads us along the sorrowful way. One step at a time, day by day, he provides what we need to move forward.

When you suffer, or walk with a loved one who suffers, God draws close. I believe he cries with us. In our times of suffering we learn God is sovereign. Not only is he in control of time and space, but he's got you. He's got you. There's a holy rest in that truth. Nothing else in life teaches us that not one thing happens to us without his knowledge quite like suffering does.

These truths don't take away the suffering or make circumstances fair. They do allow our hearts to respond to him, our great comforter and healer. In his presence, we can express anger, cry out for justice, ask for divine miracles, let ourselves have a good cry. We can begin to find hope again. Oh, for grace to trust him more.

Maybe of the double portion of everything Job received after all his suffering, the thing he valued most was the new understanding he had of God.

Traci Rhoades
Author of *Not All Who Wander (Spiritually) Are Lost*
https://www.tracesoffaith.com/

WHEN PEACE LIKE A RIVER,
ATTENDETH MY WAY,
WHEN SORROWS LIKE SEA
BILLOWS ROLL
WHATEVER MY LOT,
THOU HAST TAUGHT ME TO SAY
IT IS WELL, IT IS WELL,
WITH MY SOUL

— HORATIO SPAFFORD

What this Book is...
and What it Isn't

This isn't one of those books in which I assure you, from the comfort of my safe, suburban home, that everything happens for a reason.

This isn't one of those books that treats Christianity like a self-help regimen, in which I promise that if you live a certain way, you will earn Jesus Points that are redeemable for cash value.

This isn't a book that lectures you for suffering because you clearly have some unrecognized sin in your life.

So, what kind of book is this?

In a nutshell, this is a book for people who have heard one too many times that all things, from bankruptcy to child abuse to genocide, happen according to God's will (and the fact that they haven't throat-punched anyone for saying this is a testament to the power of the Holy Spirit).

This is a book for people who have watched a loved one slowly, painfully slip away from a terminal illness—and feel hot flashes of anger every time they see a Facebook post that praises God for healing someone else of the exact same illness.

This is a book for people who initially turned to Jesus because he offered hope in the midst of trials—but they look at other Christians around them who praise God for things like parking spaces and football championships and wonder if they are worshiping the same God.

To be sure, much ink has been spilled over the centuries about the purpose of suffering. I don't have much to contribute to that—how can I? I only have half a seminary degree in biblical counseling. While I have experienced some legitimate hardships, most of my problems can be chalked up to those of a privileged, upper-middle-class white girl. At this time, I've just broken off the seal of a new era called The Thirties. What wisdom, if any, can I offer?

I can tell you some of the reasons I became a Christian in the first place: many of which had to do with the need for a strong spiritual context in which to place the pain I felt. I needed a God who empathized with pain because he, too, had lived it.

I can tell you how my faith was deepened during some of the worst crises in my life—and how, while I wish those crises didn't happen, I am a better disciple because of them.

Some people pull away from God when life is overwhelmingly painful. I sympathize with such Christians, but I've always been the opposite: it's hard for me to feel close to God when everything is going well. I tend to open my Bible more and hound him with prayer after prayer when

I'm struggling through something. The truth is, when my life is going well, I sometimes forget to pray—even just to say, "thank you."

Not everyone will suffer the exact same way. But for most of the population, issues of financial despondency, grief, loss, and disappointment will crop up in some form or another. I am of the belief that these things happen because we live in a fallen world—not because God is testing us, punishing us, or getting some twisted pleasure out of poking us with a stick.

I suppose now would be a good time to mention that some instances of suffering—systemic, global forms of suffering rooted in human cruelty and greed, such as war, extreme poverty, genocide, rape, domestic violence, child abuse— are beyond explanation. The answers for those are above my pay grade. "Because of sin" would be the simple answer, but I'm no fan of the simple answer. Far be it from me to tell the battered wife, the assault survivor, or the neglected child that their pain can be used for good. I can't fathom being so callous.

So please know that when I use terms like "pain" and "suffering" in this book, I am referring to common setbacks that affect many of us at some point: financial strains, loss of relationships, failures, and general disappointments. I am referring to the suffering that cannot be easily explained: terminal illness, fertility issues, or homes that get swept away by hurricanes. The types of tragedies that affect the rich and the poor, the good and the bad, alike.

At no point do I want to imply that such events are *good* things. Rather, I hope to suggest that, in the midst of the wreckage, *something* beautiful can occasionally rise up.

Sometimes, though, you really have to look hard for it. With a magnifying glass.

I believe in a God who walks with us through all seasons—whose heart breaks with ours.

More to the point: I believe that the cross is the central point of Christianity—but many Christians have forgotten this.

Many of us are familiar with the command from Matthew 16:24-26: "Pick up your cross and follow me, for whoever tries to save his life will lose it, and whoever loses his life for my sake will find it."

Those are difficult words to swallow, yet we live in a culture of bedazzled crosses on necklaces, purses, and Bible covers. We seem to have forgotten that the cross is actually a torture device. True, it was eventually transformed into a symbol of hope, but many of us tend to treat it as if that's all it ever was.

I don't intend to demean anyone who has ever doubted God's goodness during a season of crisis—it's perfectly natural to do that. What I intend to do instead is try to shift our focus and reframe our mindset as we experience whatever hand we get dealt in life.

I'm not suggesting that we embrace the probability of suffering, as some legendary martyrs are said to have done. You have every right to feel hot anger at anyone who quotes James 1:2-4 at you the moment you receive the worst news of your life ("Consider it pure joy when you face trials of many kinds, because you know that the testing of your faith produces perseverance"). It's okay to be angry at God when terrible things happen. It's okay to complain. It's okay to grieve.

It's perfectly fine to pray for healing, for a better job, for safety during a dangerous storm. But it's important to remember that Jesus' desperate prayer on the night before his crucifixion to take away this cup of suffering went unanswered. If God didn't spare his begotten son from excruciating pain, how much can *we* expect to be spared?

When we pray for healing, or deliverance of some other kind, perhaps we should also consider the addendum, "But if the worst should happen, prepare me with the tools I need to get through this, and let my faith be stronger as a result."

Because everyone suffers at some point (some more than others), I've included a list of helpful books and songs in the back of this book to help get you through that process.

Our greatest power, our greatest blessing, is not found in what we gain in this life. It's not found in "winning." It's not finishing first. One of Jesus' most controversial claims is that power, glory, and strength are found in weakness; in poverty; in being lower class; in being "losers" (imagine if more politicians believed that!).

That's not to say we shouldn't strive to succeed—rather, we should aim for a poverty of spirit. We can enjoy the benefits of the things we've worked hard for without feeling entitled to or dependent on them. None of us is more deserving of a "good life" than another.

Some of us may lose our bearings during times of crisis, which is perfectly understandable. Some of us become more beautiful after a period of refinement through fire. In the following pages, I want to explore what, exactly, that looks like.

CHRISTIANS SHOULD BE SLOWEST OF ALL TO PURSUE POLITICAL DOMINANCE AND POWER OVER EVERYONE ELSE, BECAUSE WE CLAIM WE SERVE A KING WHOSE GREATEST ACT WAS LOWERING HIMSELF TO BE A SERVANT WITH THE MISSION OF DYING TO RESCUE HIS PEOPLE.

— LAURA JOHNSON.

A Tale of Two Theologies

I'm a member of the Episcopal Church, but I was born into a Reform Jewish family, which means I come from a long line of sufferers. And if there's any demographic in history that has earned the right to say, *Why me?* it's the Jews.

My family was pretty fortunate, all things considered. As far as we know, we didn't lose anyone in the Holocaust. But the ancestors on my mother's side fled to America from Polish pogroms at the turn of the 20th century. My father's side left Russia to pursue religious freedom and immigrated to America as well.

I've had the privilege of meeting a few Holocaust survivors and listening to their stories. Some escaped the camps with their lives, but their faith went up in the smoke of the crematoriums. For others, faith was the one thing that provided a modicum of hope when witnessing human cruelty at its worst.

Rabbi Harold Kushner's book, *When Bad Things Happen to Good People*, is a beloved classic for people of all religious backgrounds. For those who haven't read it—or read it a long time ago and need a refresher since the book is older than I am—Kushner asserts that God *wants* to prevent suffering from happening, but is actually incapable of stopping it—implying that perhaps God is not all-powerful.

I find it interesting that Kushner, a rabbi, comes to this conclusion, while Christians (who share the Hebrew Scriptures) claim the exact opposite: God can do whatever he wants, but often does not intervene to prevent suffering for reasons we are not meant to understand from this side of heaven.

There are times when I find Kushner's theology more comforting: God *would* stop pain and suffering if only he could, as opposed to an all-powerful being who *could* stop it but chooses not to.

Again and again, I am struck by the contrast of how suffering plays out in both religions. Jews don't typically offer concrete reasons for it other than "shit happens," while Christians embrace suffering by embracing the cross; by clinging to a God who set aside divine privileges and suffered an agonizing death, and is said to walk alongside us in the grind of our daily lives. We don't have to reach for God in our pain; he reaches down to us and can use pain for redemptive purposes.

For Christians, that's the comfort: God suffers with us. You don't have to experience the dark wilderness alone. And yet, some people ask what purpose that ultimately serves. God suffers with you, so what? How does that make the pain any less excruciating? You still have to experience it no matter what.

I see their point. And I have no answer for it.

But I understand the value of following Christ even if there are no easy answers for the pains of the present. I am drawn to a faith that claims real power is found in weakness; that the world's social order does not determine worth or virtue. Even when evil is allowed to persist, it will not have the final say.

A friend of mine told me recently about an abusive ex-boyfriend who has started stalking her. Afraid for her safety, she filed a police report. She's also looking into a private home security system. "But," she said, "Even if something happens to me—even if he kills me—he doesn't win in the end."

I suppose that's the most critical difference when it comes to the way suffering is framed in Christianity and Judaism. Jews are focused on this present life; Christians look forward to the next one, in heaven. I really struggle to do that. I struggle with the notion that true justice can only happen in a realm I can't see, much less prove. Even if lost loved ones get redeemed there, I still have to suffer through the emptiness of that loss for the rest of my life.

Which is all the more reason, I think, to work hard toward bringing God's kingdom to Earth: a process that Judaism calls *Tikkun Olam*, which can look like anything from recycling our plastics to standing up to a racist bully at a dinner party. Bringing the kingdom of God to Earth can be inconvenient and uncomfortable business.

GOD WHISPERS TO US IN OUR
PLEASURES, SPEAKS IN OUR
CONSCIENCE, BUT SHOUTS IN
OUR PAINS: IT IS HIS MEGAPHONE
TO ROUSE A DEAF WORLD.

— C.S. LEWIS.

Persecution Plays

S ome Christians complain about having to experience any discomfort at all. Others seem unable to get enough of it—or they've experienced so little genuine suffering that they have to create it.

I can't help but think of Kim Davis, the county clerk from Rowan County, Kentucky, who in 2015 refused to issue marriage licenses to same-sex couples. Consequently, she was found in contempt of court, and jailed for five days[1]. To some conservative Christians, she's a modern-day martyr, though I'm wondering why she even applied for a job that would require her to deny services to a significant portion of her customers.

I hold the same logic regarding Christian bakers who refuse to bake wedding cakes for same-sex couples, and Catholic pharmacists who refuse to issue birth control: it's not their beliefs about gay marriage or the pill that bother me. I'm bothered when people who hold those views

---

[1] "Kim Davis." *Wikipedia*, Wikimedia Foundation, 19 May 2019, en.wikipedia.org/wiki/Kim_Davis

choose professions that require regular denial of the services they were hired to do. Maybe, if you want to simultaneously be good at your job and adhere to your values, you should find a different line of work?

To me, it seems obvious that the issue at stake here is separation of church and state, not discrimination against the Christian faith. Remember, I grew up Jewish: I saw Christianity everywhere, almost to a point of conspiracy. I remember feeling threatened by my math teacher who wore a gold cross that shimmered against her blouse as she explained the Algebra lesson; I remember the perceived mockery I felt when the school bus drove past a house that had a lit-up sign proclaiming JESUS IS THE REASON FOR THE SEASON the entire month of December.

Everywhere I went, I saw signs that seemed to tell me this was Christian Country, and my presence as a Jew was merely tolerated. (For the full story of how I became an Episcopalian, read my memoir, *Confessions of a Prodigal Daughter*). I didn't deal with much in the way of explicit anti-Semitism, but I did deal with ignorance from my peers on a regular basis about Jewish holidays and what Judaism even is. I had to educate more than one public school teacher on what Yom Kippur was, so I could have my absence excused. No Christian I know has ever had to do that for their holidays.

And yet, somehow, Persecution Envy is a real thing among American Christians. It has to be, or else film companies like PureFlix wouldn't make bank on franchises like *God's Not Dead*, in which ordinary Christians find themselves in such laughably unrealistic situations of oppression that entire legal trials are devoted to "proving" that God is dead and Jesus a literary fiction. The Christian protagonists are so saccharine their dialogue gives you cavities, and the non-Christian characters are so one-dimensionally evil, they would be laughable if you didn't know that church groups were packing the theaters by the busload, earnestly believing they are watching themselves onscreen.

I know not all Christians are like this. But enough of them are that I can't do justice to the topic of suffering for the gospel without acknowledging that, in our sincere desire to be faithful, sometimes we go overboard. Meanwhile, actual minorities—people of color, Jews, the LGBT community—are watching. This is causing great damage to our witness.

The origins of this persecution complex can be traced back to 1 Peter 2:20: "For what credit is there if, when you sin and are harshly treated, you endure it with patience? But if, when you do what is right and suffer for it, you patiently endure it, this finds favor with God." Perhaps our intentions started out well enough. But in our desire to imitate Christ, we forget that these words were written at a time when Christianity was illegal—an act of rebellion against the Roman emperor—and punishable by death. Perhaps we mistakenly read these words as prescriptive, rather than descriptive.

Another possible cause of Persecution Envy could be that Christians are just too bored in America. With no systemic oppression to rally against, the only solution is to manufacture conspiracies.

I have read about Christians who speak of marital rape and domestic violence as unique crosses that the victim must bear with utmost holiness. Unfortunately, some of these Christians are pastors or administrators at seminaries, with large platforms of people who take their words as gospel.

Baptist leader Paige Patterson is reported to have once told a battered woman whose husband refused to let her go to church that, rather than leave him, she should pray for him instead. The woman came back to Patterson a few days later with two black eyes. She reportedly told Patterson, "I hope you're happy," to which he responded that he was: in her so-called "noble suffering," the husband was convinced of his need to go to church with his wife[2].

I wonder if part of the reason that some Christians are quick to assign martyr-like qualities to victims is because we don't tend to recognize patterns of abuse when we read them in Scripture. Starting in Genesis 20, with the story of Abraham and Sarah, we are witnesses to a timeline of domestic abuse. In order to avoid a famine, the couple travels to Egypt, where Abraham tells his wife to pretend she is his sister so the Egyptians don't kill him to take her for themselves as she was extremely beautiful. But when the Pharaoh lays eyes on Sarah, he demands that she become "part of his house." This is fancy Bible talk for "forced to join his harem," which means she was very likely raped.

The same happens to Esther when she was forced into a beauty pageant, and then a bedroom contest in order for

[2] Quillin, Martha. "Baptist Leader Paige Patterson Stands by His Controversial Advice to Spousal Abuse Victims." *Newsobserver*, Raleigh News & Observer, 1 May 2018, www.newsobserver.com/news/local/article210215494.html

the king to find his next wife.

We don't ever hear from Sarah or Esther, so we don't know if this these were situations they wanted to be in—but given the power imbalance between Sarah and the Pharaoh, Esther and the king, their consent is sketchy at best.

The cycle of abuse continues when Sarah turns on her handmaid, Hagar, whom she orders Abraham to impregnate (read: rape) when they can't conceive on their own. Did Hagar have a choice about sleeping with her master because her mistress was barren? We don't know; again, the power imbalance between master and servant makes consent murky, if not impossible.

But Hagar is blessed by God when she has the child, because he heard her cries in the desert when she fled Sarah's mistreatment. Is this where we get the idea that abuse must be bore with patience and endurance? Possibly.

Regarding imbalances of power that make enthusiastic consent questionable, we also have the stories of Joseph and his master Potiphar's wife, and the infamous David and Bathsheba. In a unique twist where the man is the target, Joseph was the victim of unwanted advances by his master's wife. When he refused, she cried rape, resulting in his banishment. And with David, we are told that he was "overcome with lust" when he laid eyes on the beautiful Bathsheba bathing on her rooftop, and he "ordered" her to be brought to him. Does that sound enthusiastic to you? What common woman has the ability to refuse a king—at least, without dire consequences to her safety?

Lest you accuse me of reading these stories with modern standards of morality, we see different versions of these same stories in the media all the time. Some things never change. Instead of a king approaching a commoner, we hear about presidents acting sexually with their interns, of Hollywood directors requesting inappropriate favors from actors to supposedly help them get ahead.

We are so used to reading these stories through the eyes of the victors, we don't tend to consider them from the other way around. We're so used to seeing the persecution narrative shine its spotlight on the wrong people. Thus, when we encounter survivors in our own lives, many of us don't know how to respond appropriately.

Sure, beautiful things can be born out of suffering, but that doesn't mean all suffering is created equal. Sometimes, the most Christ-like response to it is to offer a hug or a warm beverage and say, "I am so sorry that happened to you." The only ones who deserve persecution in these scenarios are the ones inflicting the abuse.

The same group of Christians who cling to unrealistic persecution narratives also seem very attached to their guns. Some even go so far as to claim that the Second Amendment, the right to bear arms, is not just a government-granted right but a God-given one[3]. I find this strange at best, and downright heretical at worst (and that's a word I don't use all that often). Violence was never supposed to

---

[3] Chumley, Cheryl K. "God-given, Not Government Granted, Guides 2nd Amendment." *The Washington Times*, The Washington Times, 29 May 2018, www.washingtontimes.com/news/2018/may/29/god-given-not-government-granted-guides-second-ame/

have a place on this planet; it only became an unfortunate staple of human life *after* the Fall.

While many tools that get turned into weapons have other useful purposes—knives are designed to cut our food into bite-sized pieces, for example—the gun only has one purpose, and that is to take life. Aside from self-defense (which I don't believe is a sin), when is killing ever justified? When is it ever okay for Christians, of all people, to celebrate it simultaneously with the cross?

In these circles, the emphasis on weakness as any sign of strength at all has been dropped completely. Russell Moore, the dean of the School of Theology at Southern Baptist Theological Seminary, wrote for *Church Leaders* about a picture of a bumper sticker he saw on Twitter that reads, "If Jesus had a gun, he'd still be alive today."[4] Is that statement meant to be read with tongue firmly in cheek? Probably. And yet, its implications are critical: weapons of destruction, not a humble spirit, are signs of strength for not just Americans, but American Christians in particular. The portrait of a stereotypical American Christian is someone (presumably white) holding a Bible in one hand, and an AK-47 in the other.

This strange love affair with weapons of mass destruction is why nothing ever gets done about the children and teachers who are gunned down in their classrooms every year.

---

[4] Moore, Russell. "What a Stupid Bumper Sticker Can Tell Us About American Christianity." *ChurchLeaders*, 26 Apr. 2019, https://churchleaders.com/pastors/pastor-articles/314862-stupid-bumper-sticker-can-tell-us-american-christianity.html

No reasonable person is suggesting that we do away with the right to own guns completely (at least, I'm not). While I can't imagine Jesus advocating the right to possess any weapon, I don't think he'd be against policies that advocate for responsible gun ownership, either. Still, the idea that this "right" to self-defense can be justified with Scripture puzzles me. And it is very likely that Jesus, with his Arab-looking features, would be a target for bullets if he were walking the streets today.

By and large, American Christianity doesn't seem to have a problem inflicting suffering as a type of refinement by gunfire, which is a very different animal from the *refinement by fire* the Bible talks about. Somehow, the message got lost in translation.

The real opportunities for harsh judgment as a result of our faith are right in front of us—we just need to shrink our scale a bit. We Christians are odd enough on our own without having to make strawmen of atheists or the ACLU.

We believe in abstinence until marriage, which made dating in college (and dating in general) really difficult for some of us.

We believe in serving the needs of the poor, which makes some politicians think we support handouts for little to no hard work.

We believe in radical forgiveness, which makes us freaks; we believe that even Hitler and Stalin could be redeemed if they genuinely repented, which makes us *insane*.

We're not interested in defining ourselves by our wealth, our achievements, or our possessions, which makes most of pop culture completely irrelevant to us.

We worship a man who didn't inquire about pre-existing conditions before he healed people; that makes us the natural enemy of insurance companies.

We are also the nemeses of white supremacists, corrupt billionaires, dictators, and sex traffickers. At least, we should be living in a way that says we are.

So, as you can see, we don't need to invent outlandish persecution fantasies. Two thousand years after the fall of Rome, we may not have to worry about being publicly executed anymore, but we shouldn't have to worry about our ability to still raise eyebrows and roll the eyeballs of society. Jesus made sure of that.

It's one thing to miss out on dating opportunities because you refuse to have premarital sex, or to get teased because your faith compels you to be selective about your entertainment choices. I think Christians in America expect that sort of difficulty. But standing up to problems in the culture at large—systemic racism, unaffordable healthcare, blaming rape victims for their assaults—is a different kind of sacrifice. At best, we end up ruining Thanksgiving dinner. At worst, your Aunt Linda might refuse to ever talk to you again.

But Jesus didn't seem afraid of exacerbating political and social divisions when he flipped over tables inside the Temple that were used for money changing. He pissed off all the wrong people—and got killed for it. Chances are if we do the same, we won't get crucified. In America, we're more likely to experience the emotional pain of gossip and severed relationships. That's never an easy thing to go through, but it's still a far cry from genuine persecution.

I wonder maybe, just maybe, if this is part of what Jesus meant when he talked about a "narrow way" in Matthew 7:13-14: "Enter through the narrow gate. For wide is the gate and broad is the road that leads to destruction, and many enter through it. But small is the gate and narrow the road that leads to life, and only a few find it." Giving lip service to following Jesus is easy, but when opportunities arrive, many Christians will slink away, not wanting to cause a scene. Not wanting to suffer more than is necessary.

IN THE HISTORY OF THE CHRISTIAN CHURCH, THE TENDENCY HAS BEEN TO EVADE BEING IDENTIFIED WITH THE SUFFERINGS OF JESUS CHRIST; PEOPLE HAVE SOUGHT TO PROCURE THE CARRYING OUT OF GOD'S ORDER BY A SHORTCUT OF THEIR OWN. GOD'S WAY IS ALWAYS THE WAY OF SUFFERING, THE WAY OF THE LONG, LONG TRAIL.

—OSWALD CHAMBERS

What I Learned During an Economic Crisis

When I first converted, one thing I immediately noticed was how common it is for Christians to praise God for every good thing that happens in their lives, even if it happened as a result of human actions. God was praised for giving someone a job, even though they were the ones who took the time to apply and show up for interviews. God was praised for healing cancer, even though the patient endured rounds of chemotherapy.

I don't want to say that God *couldn't* be responsible for those things. I believe every good thing in this life is ultimately from him. But after watching my father slowly die of Hodgkin's Lymphoma, and my husband struggle to find a job after being unexpectedly laid off, our savings draining away month after month, my mind can't help but think of everyone who isn't so lucky. Doesn't God care about them?

My life is a lot more financially stable now, but the questions still linger.

That nine-month stretch of unemployment, during

which we lived off my writer's income while digging into our savings, and occasionally accepting help from our parents, taught me a lot—though I won't deny that the biggest reason we were able to keep our house and not declare bankruptcy was because of the financial privilege we had to begin with.

And even if worse came to worse and we *did* have to sell our house, my empty-nesting mom would have welcomed us back to her house in Ohio, where we could have lived rent-free until we found new jobs and re-built our savings again. Was that God's provision for us? My best answer, honestly, is *I don't know*. But I think that depends a lot on how you define "provision."

The lessons I learned during that period of uncertainty were a mix of Christian hope—*God provides, but not always in ways we expect*—and the Jewish practices of *Tzedakah* (charity) and *Tikkun Olam* (mending the world).

The week Josh lost his job, we'd had a horrible fight in which I told him maybe we should spend time apart for a while. It was the culmination of several years of clashing as our belief systems seemed to be moving in opposite directions, and something finally set me off. I told him I could go to my mother's in Ohio and maybe, hopefully, gain some perspective there. That was what I told myself, anyway.

The reality was, I just wanted to get away. Our political differences became glaringly obvious in the months before and after Donald Trump became president. Suddenly we started arguing about Black Lives Matter and immigration and other matters of social policy that never came up when we were dating (and why would they?). In short, I felt like I didn't know him anymore. He seemed to feel the same way about me.

I was out running errands when Josh called to tell me he no longer had a job. I could tell immediately that he was about to give me bad news by the way he immediately said, "I just want you to know that I love you" when I answered the phone. Who starts a phone conversation that way if they aren't in some sort of life-or-death crisis? I imagined him lying by the side of the road, with only enough cell phone battery and life breath left to make one last call: 911 or to me. With this scenario in mind, I was prepared to yell at him to hang up and call for actual help—I didn't need to hear something I already knew if time was limited in an emergency.

I guess you could say there was a sort of death that day—a laying down of disagreements and pride and the desire to be right, not to mention the death of indulgent spending habits we had to quit cold turkey.

After the call, I drove home with the words, "This is fine" looping through my mind, like the cartoon dog in the popular Facebook meme sitting at the table drinking coffee as the kitchen around him goes up in flames. It didn't occur to me to pray right then; I suppose I was just too stunned. There would be plenty of times for desperate prayer in the future, but part of me was also afraid that if I reached out to God right then I might fall apart at the wheel and not make it home safely.

That night was a turning point in our marriage. It was a night full of tears, apologies, and promises to do better. That promise was made on both of our ends. Josh felt like a crappy husband for no longer being able to provide, and I felt like a crappy wife for not having enough of an income to keep us afloat until he found something else.

If there's one thing Josh and I have in common—something we instantly bonded over when we first became friends, before we started dating—it's dry humor. "If we're both failures," I said, measuring each word carefully, "then I guess we should stick together. No one else will want us."

"I'm in if you're still in," he replied, smiling weakly. We had agreed to be a team, for better or for worse. Unfortunately, some pretty serious "for worse" moments got dealt to us in the early years of our marriage, which I'm told are supposed to be the happiest. Or maybe they're the hardest. I'm honestly not sure which.

When our political disagreements edged closer to indictments about how compatible we were together, I called my mom, who was also seeing someone she didn't fully agree with politically, hoping she'd have some insight. She told me, "You're both looking at things from the perspective of different life experiences. I don't think you're mad at each other, you're mad about not being able to see an issue from a perspective you haven't lived. Just remember that for every Facebook post or comment, there's a complex person behind the screen you can't see. But you live with Josh—you see the whole person that he is. Do you believe he's a bad person?"

Of course he isn't. I knew that. I also knew that my mother is not someone who keeps her brutal honesty to herself: not if a dress I'm thinking of buying looks unflattering on me, and certainly not with regard to my taste in life partners, should any contenders exhibit red flags.

Long before Josh got laid off, I had automatic withdrawals set up to donate to local food banks and international rescue missions for refugees. With less money to donate, I had to re-evaluate what it means to "give." Turns out, giving your time and energy to causes can be just as beneficial as giving financially. I had to re-learn the importance of calling my senators, showing up at protests to make my voice heard, and volunteer work with the actual beneficiaries of my money.

I also had to rethink my definition of "financial security." That's a term that means different things to different people, I know.

Around month six of unemployment, a friend talked us into taking a Dave Ramsey class at a local church. Ramsey, if you've never heard of him, is an evangelical financial guru whose advice is practically gospel to a lot of people. I was a little skeptical in the beginning, especially when he called it a "baby step" to put one thousand dollars into an emergency fund[5]. I can think of at least five people off the top of my head that do not have one thousand dollars to their name, and if they did, it would immediately have to be given to rent or car payments or something else required to survive. It seemed to me that Ramsey was out of touch with how most Americans live.

But there was one thing he said that has stayed with me (and, I suppose, was worth the cost of enrollment): those who hold onto their money with an iron grip are more likely to lose it, compared to those who incorporate giving into their lives. How is that possible? The more

---

[5] "Dave Ramsey's 7 Baby Steps." *Dave Ramsey's 7 Baby Steps | DaveRamsey.com,* www.daveramsey.com/dave-ramsey-7-baby-steps#baby_step_1

money you give, the less you have in your account—that's pretty simple logic. And I don't believe in tithing for the sake of getting more back in the end, which kind of defeats the purpose of giving in the first place.

Here's the situation I think Ramsey meant (although I can't say for sure): we may have had less money than we were used to, but by focusing on what we did have rather than despairing over what we didn't, we somehow ended up becoming richer. We doubled down on our efforts to engage with our community. We had people over for game nights at our house at least once a month and requested that people bring side dishes to share (or chip in a few dollars for pizza). As more people became aware of our situation, they left the food with us rather than take home the leftovers.

At one point, a bunch of our friends chipped in money for a Target gift card, which covered our groceries for an entire month. It came with a note that thanked us for hosting them in our home. And because we could no longer afford to go out for brunch after church with that group (a regular Sunday tradition), we invested more time in one-on-one meetings with people, either in our house with coffee or out hiking in national parks.

Now that our situation has changed—Josh works at a pain management clinic while driving for Uber on the side, and my freelance career has grown considerably in the last few months—I look at money differently than I used to. This month, I admit it was jarring to look at our savings account and see a number that is much lower than what I was used to seeing at the start of our marriage. I'll be honest; it still freaks me out a little bit. I want that number to be much higher. I would feel *so much more secure* if only that number were higher.

But we have enough to cover the mortgage for this month, and the next. When the money from this week's paycheck is spent on the car payment, student loans, and groceries, another paycheck will replace it.

We're basically breaking even right now, and still don't have much for going out to eat with friends, but we're surviving. We have food in the fridge, and our two fur princesses maintained their life of luxury this whole time. If they are happy, we are *definitely* happy.

I don't share all this to make a point with some useless platitude about how true wealth is found in relationships or whatever. I'm still irked by the phrase "Money can't buy happiness," because money pays for housing and health insurance, which are two big staples for the bare minimum of happiness.

But it still remains true that money *isn't* everything. My spending habits have changed. I've been inspired to sell or give away a lot of "stuff" I thought was valuable, but turns out, I can live without it. At one point, I started selling off my wardrobe (filled with lots of "cool" overpriced items I hardly ever wore) for gas and grocery money. Thinking of all the money I spent on clothes that were well made yet overpriced, and probably held the memories of underpaid, overworked women and children in sweatshops, convinced me to never buy new clothes again. No more feeding the Capitalist Machine (but if you do need new clothes, you'll be surprised by all the name-brand clothing you can find greatly discounted and in good condition at thrift stores and on shopping apps like Poshmark).

I also learned how to be more creative in our meal planning. Meat is expensive, so I stopped buying it as often (which is better for the planet anyhow). You can make a full, satisfying meal with grilled vegetables and rice or beans. Not every meal requires more than one course, a side, and a salad. And crockpot meals freeze well, after you're sick of eating them for several days in a row. Remembering the frozen meals in your freezer when the food budget is low is as exciting as finding a $20 bill in the pocket of an old sweater.

Perhaps most importantly, having less money forced Josh and I to grow closer in ways that maybe we wouldn't have otherwise. When we first married, he was working nearly fifty hours a week at a hospital while I stayed home, writing books, doing occasional freelance editing, and making jewelry to sell on Etsy. I was happy if I made $100 per month—I didn't need to earn much more than that. When I wasn't writing, I'd sleep most of the day, hung over from the night before. My father's death was still a fresh, gaping wound.

Had Josh not lost his job, I wonder if I might ever have been motivated to get my freelance career off the ground. And yet, unfortunate though it was, it was precisely the push I needed. I searched for work on job posting sites and Facebook groups for freelancers, and in one month landed a position doing contract work for a company that writes advertisements and builds webpages for small companies. My workload started small at first, since the nature of my tasks were things I needed to be trained how to do, but by the end of the summer I was nearly able to pay the mortgage by myself.

More valuable than finally making real money was the odd thing that happened in my marriage. Instead of unemployment making things worse between Josh and I, inciting arguments about how to manage the money left in our dwindling savings account, and whether one of us should suck it up and get a job at McDonald's just to have *something* coming in, we learned how to *like* each other again.

While I want to think we could have learned that some other way, those long nine months of job searching taught us something that several sessions of marriage counseling did not. Maybe it wasn't communication skills we needed to focus on (although you can't ever have too much help with those). I wonder if something had to happen to force us to become vulnerable in front of each other again.

Until that point, the only vulnerable one in the relationship had been me. Most notably, when I was so drunk I could barely hold my own head up, and Josh was the one who held my hair back as I puked, and then put me in the shower to wash off the puke that didn't make it into the toilet. I don't want to admit how many times he did this. But he did, and still he stayed. Not because I owed him in return for all that emotional labor, but because somehow, through it all, he saw something in me. And once he was no longer able to provide for us financially—the very thing that society wants us to believe is what makes a "real man"—God saw fit to remind me of what it was I still saw in him. And what I saw was love.

I remember one afternoon when Josh called me from his new job, just as I was putting the finishing touches on a freelance article. He asked what I was up to, and I told him about my latest assignment: a series of advertisements for a company that sells tennis equipment.

Josh told me, "You know, I just want to tell you that I'm really proud of you for the way you've stepped up to help our family. You're doing an awesome job."

It's hard to say if such a compliment would have resonated nearly as much if not for what we went through the year before. Either way, I found myself beaming for days like a love-struck schoolgirl. His words were weighted by that hardship and were some of the nicest he's ever said to me.

I AM A CHRISTIAN BECAUSE I CAN'T GET OVER THE IDEA OF "GOD WITH US." BEING A HUMAN FEELS UNBEARABLE A LOT OF DAYS. I PRAY TO A GOD WHO KNOWS EXACTLY HOW THAT UNBEARABLE HUMANNESS FEELS.

— Laura Jean Truman

Requiem for a Friend

March 12, 2003 started like any normal day. I was a fourteen-year-old eighth grader, and my biggest challenge that morning was not falling asleep during my first class. I was wearing velvet track pants and sparkly Sketcher's. My binders had rainbow stickers all over them, and my backpack was bright purple.

My third period class was biology. Shortly after I sat down at my desk, an announcement came over the loud-speaker, asking the entire eighth grade class to come down to the gymnasium for an emergency assembly. Along the way, classmates were whispering to each other: "I heard it's because someone killed himself."

My curiosity was piqued, along with everyone else's. "Who was it?"

⟋⟋⟋

We met in sixth grade, in choir class. At some point during warm-ups with vocal scales, the boy next to me passed me a note: "I'm bored already." I suppressed a giggle and wrote back, "Me, too." It was text messaging before cell phones. I never thought to save the notes; now I wish I had.

Eleven years old was probably the oldest I could get away with inviting a male classmate to my house, in my room, without having it be weird. We played checkers, Topple, and other board games. We climbed the biggest tree in my backyard, and he attempted to catch me when my foot slipped on a branch, and I fell (only about five feet, thankfully). I liked him, though I don't think I thought of boys in terms of crushes yet.

Our friendship was contained to board games at my house, the tree in my backyard, and passing notes in choir for the rest of the year. We didn't interact much anywhere else, and I never had another class with him. Come to think of it, I'm not sure who else he hung out with besides me, but our social circles must never have crossed, because we stopped talking and hanging out by the year's end.

This was, of course, before cell phones and social media—even Myspace. I couldn't "like" his Facebook and Instagram posts to subtly let him know I was still interested in his life. We drifted apart, as middle school peers tend to do, but when I learned of his death, I still wondered: should I have made more of an effort?

These thoughts intensified when the school counselor addressed the eighth-grade class to talk about the importance of kindness. "You never know who might be struggling," she said. "That kid sitting by themselves at lunch might really be in need of a friend."

Despite being an introvert at heart, I took that advice

more seriously than I'd ever taken anything. Suddenly, every kid sitting alone at lunch was at risk of suicide. Every classmate who posted emo song lyrics in their away messages on Instant Messenger must have been depressed. Other kids might be overly concerned with their own friend groups and trying to be popular, but not me. I suddenly had my heart set on being the girl who went out of her way to make others feel included; every stranger was just a friend not yet met.

It churns my stomach to remember it now, but I distinctly remember writing those words down in my journal. My intentions were good, but in execution, they were absolutely terrible. My attempts to "reach out" weren't organic, and I probably irritated the heck out of more peers than I actually befriended. I don't know how obvious it was that I basically treated them as charity projects, and I can hardly blame the ones who told me, "Thanks, but no thanks" when I asked them to join me at lunch.

It would be years before I would learn that some people—my adult-self included—*prefer* eating their lunches alone.

I'm not little Miss Sarahbeth Saves the World anymore (thank God). Today, I might lean too far in the opposite direction. As a whole, people tend to irritate me. I get anxious if I'm surrounded by them for too long. I never feel quite so awkward as when I meet someone for the first time and have to introduce myself and explain that I write about theology for a living. If someone saw me eating lunch alone in a cafeteria today, I'd feel more uncomfortable if they came up and asked to sit with me than if they simply smiled from across the room.

The advice given to students left behind after a tragedy hasn't changed much. After the shooting at Marjory Stoneman Douglas High School in Parkland, Florida, students across the country protested the government's lack of action about gun control by walking out of their classes. But not everyone thought this was a worthwhile move. #WalkUpNotOut started trending on social media: the idea being that if students merely "walked up" to the lonely, standoffish kids, maybe school shootings (or any act of violence, even just against oneself) could be prevented[6].

Here's what I wish an adult had told my eighth-grade self instead: you are not responsible for the choices that other people make. Someone else's violence or self-harm is never your fault. Just be kind; don't turn a blind eye toward bullying but tell a parent or a teacher. Your main job is to be a kid, not a hero, and that's perfectly okay.

In my own struggle with depression, I appreciate the occasional text message from people who haven't heard from me in a while and are simply "checking in." I love getting photos of people's pets. I always appreciate offers to meet for coffee even if I sometimes lack the energy to put on

---

[6] Spencer, John, and John Spencer. "Five Reasons the 'Walk Up, Not Out' Meme Is So Problematic." *Medium,* Medium, 15 Mar. 2018, https://link.medium.com/QwmClD9ReZ

clothes, much less leave my house. Little things become big things.

How the depressed mind works can't be fully explained if you haven't walked through depression yourself. Asking a person what they need can be helpful, but the depressed person sometimes doesn't know what that is; or maybe it's multiple things at once. Saying to someone, "We're going to get dressed up and go out tonight" could be a nice gesture for some, or it could put others on the spot and create unnecessary anxiety.

Depression is managed by a multitude of techniques: no two sufferers self-care alike. As a married woman with depression, I can attest that trying to come up with the magic words to make it all go away, as my husband (God bless him) has tried to do, doesn't only not work—it's annoying as hell. But being present, giving people the space and permission to feel, or cry, or to simply say "I'm sorry you're going through this" can be a game changer.

So how do you prevent someone you love from harming themselves? Ultimately, you can't. But you can present yourself as a safe person; someone who listens, and doesn't plaster over the pain with "Have you tried just being positive for once?" You can make baby steps toward creating a culture that doesn't respond to mental illness with harmful stigmas.

With the help of my adorable cats napping in sunlight, I started talking about having depression on Instagram. I started reading and responding to posts tagged with #EndTheStigma. I reached out to authors and bloggers who wrote about depression and thanked them for their work. I never take it for granted if someone sends me a private message thanking me for my willingness to be transparent about something so dark and complicated.

There is probably more that I could do, but I don't pressure myself to do everything. There is only one Savior; I am not him.

When I was in the middle of my Save The World phase, I did manage to do something right.

I met G's sister, K, at the funeral. A year ahead of me in school, I knew K and I had some friends in common, but it's hard to say if we ever would have crossed paths any other way. I wouldn't say I knew her before then, but rather, I knew *of* her. Still, as she stood in the receiving line of guests with her parents and younger sister, I gave her a hug. Or maybe she gave me a hug, and I reciprocated. Being one of those moments where no single move is the right one (though there are about a million *wrong* ones), I don't recall if I said anything to her, though she would tell me later that if she had a penny for every time she heard "I'm so sorry" that year, she could have her student loans paid off today.

About a year after G's death, my dad's cancer returned. The first time he was diagnosed with Hodgkin's Lymphoma, when I was in seventh grade, the disease had been growing for several years, but wasn't so far advanced that surgery alone could not treat it. This time, toward the end of ninth grade, surgery and chemotherapy were necessary.

I'm not sure what prompted me to think of K and her family at this time, since cancer and suicide are two very different tragedies that provoke very different responses in people. Society doesn't tend to pity suicide victims the same way they do cancer patients. They see the former as self-inflicted, not realizing that depression is a disease, too.

But in my mind, I figured I could relate to K in at least two ways, which I explained when I called her on the phone after school one day. After telling her about my dad's diagnosis, I asked her, "How do you keep going on when your life has been turned upside down?"

And later, "How do you keep from throwing things when people say stupid stuff that's supposed to make you feel better?" This made her laugh. Despite the differences in our sufferings, we bonded over one universal fact that eclipsed them both: when something goes unexpectedly, terribly wrong, the people you turn to for support some-times end up making a bad situation worse. They don't mean to, of course—but if someone is stepping on your toes, it doesn't matter whether they meant to or not. The point is, your toes still freaking hurt.

We both agreed "Everything happens for a reason" is the worst well-intentioned-but-not-helpful response. We reasoned that the next time someone said that to us, we'd ask what that reason is… and then try to suppress laughter as the person's face crumpled with awkward realization that they said something dumb.

That one phone call, which lasted from midafternoon until I heard shouts from downstairs to join the dinner ta-ble, instigated a friendship that persists to this day. Its frui-tion included notes passed to each other between classes (again, back before text messages existed) in which we vented all the feelings we couldn't tell anyone else, be-cause our old friends just didn't want to deal with us being sad all the time. It led to meals delivered to my house when Dad's chemo made him too weak to cook; annual messages on March twelfth that said, "Hey, how are you?" A sentiment that could be sent on any day, even though we both knew what the real significance was.

Those messages evolved from handwritten notes on notebook paper to memos left on answering machines to messages via AOL Instant Messenger, and, finally, to text messages via iPhone. No matter where I am in the world—my home state of Ohio, a semester abroad in Italy, or present-day Colorado—and no matter which medium of technology is most popular at the time, I never miss a March twelfth. And she checks in with me on September twenty-fifth.

I'm profoundly grateful that *something* beautiful came from the aftermath of two lost lives, cut short too soon. But if K and I could have our way, of course we'd rather go back to the way things were—the way they ought to have been—with Dad and G still alive, even if it meant that we might never have become more than acquaintances at school.

Spinning crap into fertilizer doesn't require something terrible to happen in order for something good to take place, which is why I find that sentiment more useful than "Everything happens for a reason."

If there's any "reason" at all for what happened to Dad and G, I can name at least two of them. For Dad, it was drawing the genetic short straw when it came to genes. As for G, maybe there was too much of a stigma surrounding mental illness in order to reach out for help. There are some things I will never know—many things his own family might never know.

In both situations, there is much to be prepared for harvest. There is research for cures to help fund, hurting people still alive that can be helped. There are myths to bust ("Just focus on the positive and you won't feel so sad"; "You won't get cancer if you cut out processed foods and eat a plants-based diet").

I am eager to see what grows.

I WAITED PATIENTLY FOR THE LORD. HE TURNED TO ME, AND HEARD MY CRY.

PSALM 40:1

Zoey

To be perfectly honest, I'm not sure what I was thinking when I initially moved to Colorado. I was tired of Ohio weather, yes. I was looking for a new start in that dramatic way of headstrong twenty-somethings. For some reason, I thought seminary was the place to do that: a conservative bubble of mostly cradle Baptists who had never met a person with beliefs that skewed toward liberal.

I majored in divinity for the first semester, only to switch to biblical counseling when it became clear that Hebrew and I were just not meant to be friends (I tried—I really did). Because "Chaplain Caplin" sounded *so cool*, I just assumed that was the path God obviously planned for me.

But in between realizing how many people in my program believed depression and anxiety were sins to be confessed rather than mental illnesses in need of treatment, and dealing with a personal faith crisis after expressing doubts about the wrong issues in front of the wrong people, I quit. I only lasted a year and a half, with nothing to show for it but a few thousand dollars of debt and a diagnosis of agnosticism.

By the time I withdrew from all my classes, my then-boyfriend, Josh, had already accepted a job an hour north of Denver. He was in the process of driving a U-Haul across the country as I drove a borrowed pick-up truck across Denver, away from the seminary campus and into a three-bedroom apartment with two roommates I met online, who for some reason had no qualms about accepting a seminary dropout with no job or plans for her future.

All that is to say, by the time Josh proposed, we decided we were too used to Colorado's 300 days of sunshine compared to Cleveland's 300 days of rain. We made our first home in a small apartment in Greeley, and within days of returning from our honeymoon, our hearts were stolen by a little girl named Zoey.

To be clear, Zoey is a feline. At the time we met her, she was barely four months old, and as snuggly and adorable as any kitten could be. Her grey and white stripes, pink nose, and pleasant little chirps immediately grabbed Josh's attention at the shelter. I was on the other side of the "cat room," falling in love at first sight with an eight-week-old mini panther, whom I named Catniss Everclean. Josh and I met up in the middle, each holding our new best friend. Our family was officially complete.

Despite being from different litters, the little babies became instant BFFs from the moment they were placed in the same carrier on the drive home. During our first winter as a married couple, the "kitten littles," as we called them, were intertwined with each other on the couch, separating only to eat their meals and use the litter box. If "adorable" had a picture definition, theirs would be it.

It was sometime around Zoey's first birthday that we noticed what looked like a rash—or maybe hives—on her sweet little face. I thought it might be a reaction to the aerosol spray I used in the bathroom where their litter box was kept, so I stopped using it. When the hives didn't go away, I tried changing brands of litter. I finally made an appointment at the vet when she started losing fur on her hind legs and developed bald spots on the top of her head. Whatever it was, it was starting to look serious.

Luckily for us, Colorado is home to one of the best schools for veterinary care. It took less than twenty seconds for the vet tech to look at our girl's face and say, "Looks like allergies. We'll run some tests, but I bet she's allergic to whatever you're feeding her."

The vet wasn't wrong. Switching to another commercialized brand wasn't an option, since mainstream pet food companies all use chicken, beef, or fish flavors in their food. As fate would have it, our girl is allergic to *all* of those things—the very substances that nature intended for her to eat. This cat failed out of Evolution 101.

Our solution was to switch Zoey to a prescription diet, which contained "minced proteins"—small enough bits of specialized meats like duck and venison, which would be enough to satisfy her biological protein requirement, but not enough to cause her to keep breaking out. The rest of the ingredients were vegetables and soy.

"I can't believe this," I lamented to Josh after entering our credit card number to order an eight-pound bag of hypoallergenic prescription food online. "Our Ohio friends think we're hippies for living in the first state to legalize weed, and now we have a cat who's practically vegan."

According to some websites I researched, ostrich

meat is another option for parents of hypoallergenic kitties. You order it online, and it arrives frozen at your door, and you cook it yourself in vegetable broth. Some people commented on a message board that they preferred this to canned food, because they could know exactly which ingredients were going into their babies' bellies. I love cats as much as the next crazy cat lady, but... frozen *ostrich meat*? How could they even tell it was real ostrich? God help me, I'm not *that* extra.

We started Zoey on her new diet, which went well for a few weeks. Praise the Lord, she didn't hate it, and her skin started to clear up. But the chunks of baldness remained—and new ones started sprouting on her back and head. So back to the vet she went—this time, she was referred to a *cat dermatologist* (who knew that was a thing?), who ran more tests. I found myself hoping that this perpetual draining of our checking account would lead to a diagnosis; at least if we could name the problem, we could work toward a solution.

"It's a good thing you're cute," I whispered to Zoey as we sat in the waiting room to discuss the test results. "You don't pay rent, you don't contribute to the grocery budget, but you sure are lovable." She responded to this by head-butting my hand, the vibration of her purrs settling my nerves and warming my heart.

At this point, her appearance would probably render her unadoptable if she were still at the shelter: the skin above her eyes was red and angry looking, the bald spots on her body more obvious than ever.

And yet, she is easily the cuddliest, most affection-hungry critter I've ever cared for. Like a dog, she greets Josh and I at the door when we come home and insists on sleeping between us at night. Meanwhile, her sister Catniss is the more stereotypically cat-like of the two. She enjoys human company, but at a distance—and only on her terms. Zoey, perhaps conscious of how unusual and expensive she is to care for, can't get enough of us... or anyone else who comes into the house, including the plumber. I have never seen a cat purr at a vet tech drawing blood before.

Finally, we had a diagnosis: not only does Zoey have food allergies, she also has psoriasis, requiring an entirely separate treatment plan. At just a year and a half old, she'd racked up hundreds of dollars in tests, biopsies, and medications. With Josh's job at a reputable hospital, we could afford it all without having to live off of Ramen noodles, but *good grief*, she was high maintenance. I can't say I'd harbor any judgment for a family that had to return her to the shelter because they couldn't afford her special needs, much as they might wish they could.

Starting that day, we put Zoey on her new treatment plan. She had to have drops of skin medication put in her wet food. When she refused to touch it, we were told to put the medication into a syringe and shoot it into her mouth instead. This was a two-person job: Josh, the stronger one, would hold her, and I'd administer the drugs. After she peed on me one too many times (to which Josh gloated, "Haha, you're a real parent now, you got peed on!"), we decided we couldn't do that anymore. It was traumatizing for all of us, and I was afraid of destroying Zoey's inherent good faith in humans by having her think we were torturing her.

In the meantime, I settled on less effective treatment measures, like sponge baths with medicated shampoo. This she wasn't happy about but tolerated. The constant itchiness had to be taking a toll on her feline sanity, so much that she barely made a sound as I dipped her into a tub of warm water and dabbed her affected areas with a sponge of special shampoo. I'd do this a few times a day, several times a week—sometimes as late as two in the morning, when the saddest, most pathetic whimpering woke me up, and Josh and I engaged in that timeless battle all parents know: "I got up for her last. No, I did. No, *I* did. Fine, I'll do it."

To people who think cats and dogs are "just pets," all this may seem ridiculous. I admit to rolling my eyes at the absurdity of it all—I mean, of all the cats at the shelter, how in the *world* did we end up with one so... so *unique*? I don't want to say "broken" or "defective," because such words really undermine the spirit of this sweet girl who has, believe it or not, brought joy and laughter into our home during some very dark times.

When we received a call from the vet telling us about a new ointment that had reported positive results in animals like Zoey, we figured, Why not? Might as well. That was the medication that turned our cat-crazy lives around. Used regularly, it works well enough that we can keep her off of steroid injections, which we'd reluctantly used for her worst outbreaks.

Zoey, of course, hates the medicine, which has to be refrigerated. I don't think she likes the coldness very much. She'll run away after we dab the clear, non-fragranced stuff on her face and feet, her tail poufy and defiant, and hide under our bed for several minutes. But she'll return about five minutes later, chirpy and affectionate as ever. It's as if she's saying thank you to us, knowing full well that another family might have returned her to the shelter, or worse, had her euthanized.

On the first anniversary of my father's death, she woke me up with kisses all over my face. Whenever I'm in tears, she's the first to jump in my lap and make biscuits: kneading her white paws into my thighs, never breaking eye contact with me as she tells me, *It's okay, Mom. I know that life is unfair.*

Of all the people life could possibly be unfair to... well, food allergies and skin problems are a pain in general, and I wouldn't wish either on anyone. But is there anything as senseless as both those conditions in a *kitty*, who can't comprehend why she's uncomfortable? I don't get it. And I'm absolutely certain that, contrary to what the friends of the biblical character Job suggested when painful boils covered his body, I don't think Zoey's skin problems are because of unconfessed sin in her life.

I never regretted my decision to come out to Colorado more than I did during the Unemployment Season. Not only did I owe several thousand dollars in student loan debt, but housing here was so expensive compared to Ohio. If we had stayed there, maybe Josh would have had a better job. We'd also be closer to our families and all our old friends. It seemed so obvious that that was where we belonged, grey skies, terrible winters and all.

And yet... I look into the sweet, sleeping face of our fur princess, now four years old, wrapped in a blanket on the couch, and perfectly comfortable because we finally found a treatment plan that works. She is living her best life—the one she deserves. I am confident, despite all the extra hardship, that we made the right life choices after all.

YOU INTENDED TO HARM ME,
BUT GOD INTENDED IT FOR GOOD
TO ACCOMPLISH WHAT IS NOW
BEING DONE, THE SAVING OF
MANY LIVES.

GENESIS 50:20

Inconvenient Reasons

Decent people would never say these things to someone in a crisis, but if you really stop and think about it, some forms of sufferings do have specific reasons behind them:

That tornado demolished your house despite it not being tornado season because your state continues to support politicians that deny that climate change is real.

Your child died inside her classroom because the legislatures who hold the power to tighten gun laws have been bought by the NRA.

The college girl was raped because her date was raised to believe that her acceptance of a drink at a bar entitled him with rights to her body.

The hard-working African American student who could have been the first of her family to go to college had her spot bought out by a wealthy white family who bribed the admission's office, so their kid with an SAT score of negative seven could get in.

Your curable disease will end up killing you because the life-saving drugs cost more than your rent, and insurance won't cover them.

White people benefit from white supremacy. Men benefit from patriarchy. Rich people benefit from a social framework that punishes the poor for being poor. Even those of us who try to be environmentally conscious will end up contributing to the planet's destruction somehow.

Some Christians will say that your suffering is a result of unconfessed sin in your life. But consider this: it may not be your own sin causing you to suffer. Sometimes people suffer from *everyone's* unrepented sin: the sins of the human race.

LET NOTHING DISTURB YOU,
LET NOTHING FRIGHTEN YOU.
ALL THINGS ARE PASSING AWAY;
GOD NEVER CHANGES.
PATIENCE OBTAINS ALL THINGS.
WHOEVER HAS GOD LACKS
NOTHING.
GOD ALONE SUFFICES.

— SAINT TERESA OF AVILA

God is the Bar

On Facebook, I'm part of a private group for people who have left extremist, toxic Christian environments, and are either looking to practice Christianity in a healthier way or have left religion completely behind. Regardless of whether or not they still believe, many people find comfort in sharing memes that expose the hypocrisy of mainstream Christian views, or screenshots of text messages from well-meaning friends or relatives (with the names blurred out) quoting Bible verses about how God redeems suffering.

Those messages are bothersome not just because they are often unsolicited, but because the entire idea of "redeeming suffering" comes off as ludicrous once one takes off the Christian lenses. What kind of good God lets suffering happen in the first place, many have asked rhetorically. What kind of God required the butchery of his own son in order to be "saved"?

Christianity, many have concluded, is not only an outdated system, but a barbaric one.

Truth be told, I completely understand why people feel that way. Perhaps it all would make more sense if we still lived in a culture of ritual sacrifice, but that's not our world anymore (not in America, anyway). Those of us who find some meaningful way to cope with suffering often do so because we have no health insurance or money to fix the problem, not because we see spiritual value in it. We suffer because we have no other option to avoid it.

I am one of those people. Sometimes I wonder if I latch on to Christianity not because it all makes perfect logical sense, but because even with antidepressants, I'll still have days when hopelessness physically hurts. Maybe I latch on to Jesus because I need all this philosophical talk of redemptive suffering to be real to me in order to see another day.

Scientists and psychologists have discovered a link between creativity and depression. This doesn't strike me as surprising, considering the number of celebrities who have been outspoken about having it: Robin Williams, Kristen Bell, Ellen DeGeneres, and Jim Carrey, to name a few[7]. What *does* strike me as surprising is just how *funny* some

---

[7] "Slideshow: Pictures of Celebrities With Depression." *WebMD*, WebMD, www.webmd.com/depression/ss/slideshow-depression-celebs

of the most famous depression-sufferers are. Indeed, some of the best performers who leave audiences rolling out of their seats with laughter have suffered some of the most debilitating hopelessness you can imagine. Some have even died by suicide or attempted it more than once.

Where is the connection between creativity and depression? Creative types, be they artists, performers, or writers, are thought to be more sensitive than the average person[8]. They tend to be extreme empaths who feel things on a deeper level than most. This depth of feeling is what makes for moving, award-winning performances, but also a great deal of inner torment.

That's a generalized theory. Others may be able to point to something more specific in their childhood, like abuse or neglect. Or perhaps they have always felt "different" than their peers somehow.

I actually had a doctor explain this to me once. I was always changing up my medications as a kid, in an attempt to find the magic one that would treat depression, anxiety, and obsessive-compulsive order without making me too tired to stay awake in class, or gain an unhealthy amount of weight, or mess with my body in some other way.

Because I saw this doctor so often, he would ask what I had been doing for fun lately. Even then, I was awkward with small talk, so my mom answered for him: "She's involved in figure skating competitions. She loves choreographing her own routines!"

"That's interesting," the doctor replied. "A lot of my

---

[8] "A Little Weird? Prone to Depression? Blame Your Creative Brain." *Psychology Today*, Sussex Publishers, www.psychologytoday.com/us/blog/prescriptions-life/201204/little-weird-prone-depression-blame-your-creative-brain

patients who have similar conditions are also into creative activities." I came away from that appointment with the understanding that I was creative *because* I suffered from mental illness. I not only loved figure skating but also writing poems and stories. I'd already written dozens of "books" from construction paper, stapled at the spine, which were proudly displayed on Mom's dresser.

If I could somehow be cured of my mental illnesses, would I no longer enjoy any of those things? Or would I no longer be as good at them?

Today, my writing is primarily focused on my conversion from Judaism to the Episcopal Church, but I still get emails from time to time about some of my older freelance writings that address mental illness, as well as rape culture and everyday sexism. I don't take those messages lightly. To hear from other survivors that they feel understood by my words is no small thing. Those messages remind me that I don't necessarily have to do something "big" or become a household name in order to make the world better. Maybe I will impact more lives composing freelance articles through tears than I will by writing books about Jesus. I don't know if this is what I'm "meant" to do, but I've proven a certain knack for it. Is my depression the driving reason for that?

It's just one item on a growing list of questions I plan to ask God one day.

I talk a lot about finding contentment in the midst of pain, which sounds lovely and poetic, but how true would it be for me if I ran out of anti-depressants and had no means to refill them?

This happened to me not too long ago, when Josh was unemployed. The pills I'd been taking, a ridiculous expense even when Josh had a good job with good insurance, had run out—even after I stretched them out as far as possible by taking them every other day, and then every two days. Our financial priorities with the money we had left were for our mortgage, groceries, and car payments. At that point we'd already borrowed a few hundred dollars from our parents so we could buy plane tickets to spend the holidays with them. Mom was paying for sessions with my therapist. I just couldn't bring myself to ask her for more money; not when my condition wasn't immediately life threatening, like running out of insulin would be.

I don't need medicine, I thought. *I have Josh; I have faith. I can get through this.* It's just a temporary season until Josh has a job again. How hard could it be?

Well. Let's just say that if I run out of medicine again one day, maybe because of a zombie apocalypse or some other Armageddon-like catastrophe, I'll be the first to offer myself up as a sacrifice so as not to be a drain on resources.

I had been sober for months, and swiftly broke that streak by consuming every bit of alcohol we had left: straight vodka, liquor, cheap white wine. Because my tolerance wasn't what it used to be, I promptly threw it all up, and then slept for about twenty-some hours. I didn't just have thoughts of suicide; I actively dreamed about it.

One night, I went looking for the switchblade we used for opening boxes when we first moved into our house. Josh, always a step ahead of me, already hid it—along with other sharp objects. I railed with all my body and might like the children in the viral "Reasons my toddler is crying" Buzzfeed post. Nothing could comfort me. My feverish mind couldn't stop spinning long enough to take in my surroundings and practice "being present," as my therapist likes to suggest, let alone pray.

Where was God in all that? Where was that hard-earned patience in times of trials I'd been reading about, and believed was attainable? Or does it only work when I have Effexor and Xanax running through my veins?

On more lucid days, I'm not positive it was faith that sustained me, so much as white-knuckling minute by minute, hour by hour, until another day was gone, and I could sigh with relief that I had made it—albeit barely.

Not surprisingly, once Josh was hired again, I got my medication back. The world had color once again. Food tasted better. I could savor the words in my favorite books, take joy in my sacred space of the house with a purring cat in my lap, and just savor being alive.

But I also felt like a failure. Worse, I felt like a hypocrite. Without a husband holding me back (sometimes literally), what would have happened to me? Why wasn't faith enough to sustain me?

It's not that I don't believe depression is a legitimate illness. It may very well be that God offers his peace not by zapping the condition away, which he could, but by giving us resources to make medication for people like me who need it.

This is exactly what I would say to someone who feels the same concerns about their own mental illness. I would assure them that there is nothing wrong with their faith, that they aren't weak, or hypocritical—no more than a person of faith who develops cancer or diabetes. Yet for some reason, I have a hard time extending that same grace to myself.

You know that expression, "Truth doesn't care about your feelings"? God can still redeem this suffering even if I'm in a place where the whole concept seems ludicrous. He can still work even if I'm convinced he's given up on me.

What's more, my limited view from behind the curtain doesn't show the full picture that God sees. While I am barely holding on for dear life, I don't know what is happening behind the scenes. I have no way of knowing that redemption isn't just around the corner. Even white knuckling my way to wellness is better than giving up, and a low bar of success is better than no bar at all. Sometimes God is the bar.

I AM NOT SAYING THIS OUT OF NEED, FOR I HAVE LEARNED TO BE CONTENT REGARDLESS OF MY CIRCUMSTANCES. I KNOW HOW TO LIVE HUMBLY, AND I KNOW HOW TO ABOUND. I AM ACCUSTOMED TO ANY AND EVERY SITUATION TO BEING FILLED AND BEING HUNGRY, TO HAVING PLENTY AND HAVING NEED. I CAN DO ALL THINGS THROUGH CHRIST WHO GIVES ME STRENGTH.

PHILIPPIANS 4:13

Go Take a Shower

There's a lot of advice out there about how to conquer your problems and live your "best life." I've never been entirely certain about what that means. How to become rich and famous? How to be great-looking and best dressed? I have no idea.

Just perusing the Self-Help section at Barnes and Noble, I notice lots of titles that seem to make those promises. If only I can just pull myself up by my bootstraps (assuming I was born with sturdy bootstraps I am physically able to pull), I can do just about anything.

Granted, I have not read every self-help book out there, so I can't say with any certainty that the authors of these books were all born into completely privileged existences, with no hardship whatsoever. I can't say that none of them have ever known pain or disappointment.

And yet. Sometimes, their messages just feel empty. Like a key ingredient is missing.

I may sell enough books to afford the expensive bag. Maybe one day I'll be able to fly first class to any country in the world. I might someday have thousands of adoring

Instagram followers who can't "like" my posts fast enough.

And yet. When moments of suffering come—and they will—what hope will those things offer me?

I think of my father, who made enough money as a traveling tradeshow manager to support his family and take us on vacation every year—but he hated just about every minute of that successful job. His real goal in life, the thing that "sparked joy," was to coach high school track and be a mentor to the boys he coached. Ironically, he was only able to achieve that goal when illness cut his career short and he had to retire.

We live in a world that measures worth by outward success. There are publishing houses that wouldn't give me a contract because my online platform isn't big enough, no matter how well I can write, or how meaningful my engagements are with the five Instagram followers who interact the most with my content.

As of now, I'm in great physical health. But how will I feel when I look at my list of goals and dreams and I'm too physically weak to accomplish them? What if I were to be measured by the things I *didn't* achieve—the bestseller lists I didn't make, the boxes of unsold books in my trunk?

I've read books and blogs that encourage me to "just be positive" and wash my face or save screenshots of my favorite Amazon reviews people wrote about my books to visit when I'm feeling down. But in the face of real suffering, I'm not sure those things will be enough.

The self-help gospel wants me to believe I am awesome and capable of anything. If I just believe in myself, the universe will let good things happen to me. I am all for healthy self-esteem, but I also advocate for healthy humility. Sure, I have good qualities and talents, but I am not entitled to good things because of them. That is a straight-up lie.

Sometimes, trying to be happy makes me feel worse. Sometimes, trying to "be positive" makes me snap. I am done trying to make "the universe" bend to my will and give me what I want. And that actually makes me feel pretty relieved.

When you are hurt, it's okay to feel the pain. It's okay to be upset. When you witness injustice in the world, it's okay to be angry. It's okay to feel helpless in the face of systemic unfairness and realize that you can't tear it down on your own. Those are appropriate, healthy responses to the reality that we live in.

That's not to say that you should give up and quit trying. Just that we should keep our perspective in check.

Self-help talk, pop psychology—it's called many things, but it is its own kind of gospel. It preaches a simple, practical, "The only one standing in your way is you" kind of mindset, which many people find helpful.

On its face, there's nothing wrong with that advice. But for people like my father, whose limitations were beyond his control, or the mother whose child was taken from her at the border and is helpless to get her back, is this advice just a slap in the face? Is it loving? Or is it cruel?

How can Jesus' message of perseverance in suffering be useful to everyone—the sick, the dying, the impoverished, the victimized?

I'm asking because I have no idea. But I do believe that his message was meant to be universal, not just for upper-middle-class white people with money and privilege.

On the flip side, what of those who *want* to be defined by their suffering—the ones who live with a perpetual victim mentality? The ones who are always looking for sympathy and pity, but have no intention of solving any of the problems within their power to solve?

Again, I have no idea. But I believe Jesus' message is also for those who wield weakness like a weapon to be perceived as strong when they aren't. I realize it's impossible for even the most down to earth self-help guru to relate to everybody, and you can't preach what you don't know. Hence why I find the biblical gospel to be more reliable.

When Jesus was being crucified, the Roman soldiers taunted him. They challenged him to get down from the cross if he was really God. And yet, he didn't. I think about that a lot. Every time my life goals (arguably less impressive than offering myself as a sacrifice for the world's sins) don't pan out as expected, I am reminded of the glory found in "losing." I remind myself of the power of weakness. If my life is any kind of illustration, it's possible to learn more and grow through "failure" than success.

The gospel of self-help may say you CAN go back for

that degree, you CAN have a "beach body." For some people, though, there are financial, medical, or other valid reasons why such things are not possible. It's not wrong to have big dreams, but as a society, I think we have a tendency to put success on a pedestal.

Dad had a revolving door of visitors during his final weeks of life. Everyone from the butcher at the grocery store to the local bank tellers to the vet techs who treated our dogs from puppies to adulthood came to see him. And they didn't just pop in, drop off a casserole and leave, either— they pulled up chairs around his hospital bed and sat for hours at a time chatting with him. His influence reached far and wide even when he could no longer walk.

That's something I don't see happening for me in my final stretch if I ever need at-home hospice care. I have two close friends and a smart mouth. My personality has never "lit up a room." If anything, when I enter a room, I hope no one turns to look at me, and at parties, I immediately start looking for the household pet to play with. Dad had a certain power in weakness that I don't have on my best days.

According to the self-help gospel, Dad "lost the fight," or the battle, or whatever euphemism you give to cancer. There's so much he didn't get to accomplish. He didn't get to walk his only daughter down the aisle at her wedding. He'll never meet his grandchildren. He didn't get to grow old with my mom.

But once we learned his time was going to be cut

short, we had talks to resolve old conflicts that might have led to estrangement if he had lived to be ninety. Suddenly, none of our previous conflicts mattered. He may have lost his life, and I will feel the ache of that loss for the rest of mine. But we gained something, too, during that time, which I now look back on with happy tears instead of ugly ones—something I don't think would have happened otherwise.

It takes a strong person to still be okay with themselves when they fall short, to not allow those failures to define who they are. But where does that strength come from? That is the real question. If the source is finite, or dependent on outward achievement, is it real? Is it stable? Will it last beyond the season's current trends? Is it possible that maybe real strength comes from recognizing that we are, in fact, *not* the center of our own lives?

Most importantly, will that source sustain you when everything else is taken, or will it disappoint you because you have nothing tangible left to offer?

HE'S NOT SAFE, BUT HE'S GOOD.

— C.S. LEWIS

On Choosing Your Own End

Brittany Maynard was a seasoned traveler, philanthropist, wife, and daughter who was diagnosed with terminal brain cancer in January of 2014. Originally from California, she moved with her family to Oregon, which has a "death with dignity" law, allowing terminal patients to die via doctor-assisted suicide. She wrote an article titled "My Right to Death With Dignity at 29" for CNN, and chose to die on November 1, 2014, by taking a pill from her doctor[9].

In the five years since her death, seven states have legalized medically assisted suicide. Despite its title, the official cause of death on Brittany's death certificate was listed as a brain tumor. In several interviews with the press before her scheduled death, Brittany stated that she didn't want die, but rather wanted to avoid pain, to spare herself and her family as much unnecessary suffering as possible.

Because my father was also dying that same year, I

---

[9] "Brittany Maynard." *Wikipedia*, Wikimedia Foundation, 1 May 2019, en.wikipedia.org/wiki/Brittany_Maynard

followed Brittany's story with great interest. Though I didn't know her, I found myself mourning her death when it hit the news because her struggle greatly mirrored my father's. Both had strong ties with their families and communities and died far too soon.

I'm morbidly fascinated by expressions like "unnecessary suffering" and "death with dignity," mainly because of what their inverses imply. Is there such a thing as *necessary* suffering? Is there such a thing as *undignified* death? If so, what do those things look like? Is the person who dies calmly and resolutely more heroic than the one who dies kicking and screaming?

As a family, we had that difficult conversation about "death with dignity," however it's defined. At that point, there was no question that Dad was dying. There was no last-ditch hope for a miracle cure. We were in the end stages. The newspaper obituary had been written (with Dad's seal of approval), and the funeral songs had been selected. Dad was bedridden and dependent on pain pills to remain lucid. We didn't quite know what the last days would look like, but according to the hospice nurses, he'd likely lose consciousness for several hours or even days before passing away.

That's pretty much what happened. Dad decided not to die early and was in a comatose state for eleven days before his heart finally stopped. He chose this path not because he believed it was God's job to decide when his life ended, but because he didn't want to lose any time he had left with his family.

But his end was erratic, disturbing, and full of senseless shouting and delirium. He wasn't my father anymore; he didn't recognize any of us before finally losing consciousness. It's hard to know for sure what he was aware of and what he wasn't. We continued playing his favorite songs, holding his hands, and telling him we loved him, just in case.

I'll be honest and admit that those last eleven days were some of the most traumatic of my life. In debating assisted suicide, part of Dad's motives weren't just about sparing himself pain, but also my mom, brother, and me. He didn't want us to watch him literally waste away.

There was also a bit of all-too-human pride involved in considering assisted suicide. Dad didn't want us to deal with emptying his colostomy bag or moving his body to avoid bedsores. If that's what is meant by "dignity," it makes a lot of sense, since we spend the majority of our lives taking care of our own private bathroom-related business. It can be humiliating to have your spouse, who knew you when your abs were flat and your head was full of hair, to have to do those things for you.

Of course, love is big enough—*should* be big enough—to accept those duties with grace. Still, it's not something any of us ever hope we have to do.

I wish I could have been spared witnessing some of the things I did during those eleven days. At the same time, the choice had to be Dad's, and whatever he wanted, we would have done.

I'm sure many people who criticized Brittany Maynard's final act have never been in her shoes or known anyone who has. But not all her critics spoke from ignorance. Kara Tippetts, a Christian author and blogger who was also dying from cancer, wrote a letter to Brittany urging her to reconsider because "God is present in pain." Kara also wrote that dying sooner than God intended would "rob" her family of the opportunity to love her, and that there could still be beauty in the midst of suffering[10].

It's hard to argue with the opinion of someone who also has firsthand knowledge of dying slowly from disease. Kara's words were formed not from a place of self-righteous judgment, but from shared experience, and I want to believe them with every fiber of my being.

But is that universally true of all suffering—that there is beauty to be found in it, if only you look hard enough? Can that be said to rape survivors, domestic violence sufferers, or starving children? What if we end up triggering the abuse survivor and chasing her away from Christianity forever by unintentionally promoting "I only hurt you because I love you" rhetoric?

The Christian view of suffering, in a nutshell, is that it can bring us closer to Christ, even if "closer" means going straight to heaven and bypassing the rest of our lives on earth. It means we do not suffer alone, whether we are taken tomorrow or left to survive another few decades. In either scenario, there is no easy peace.

---

[10] Jessup, John. "'God Is Present in Pain:' Kara Tippetts' Heroic Cancer Fight Retold in New Film." *CBN News*, 21 Mar. 2019,
https://www1.cbn.com/cbnnews/us/2019/march/god-is-present-in-pain-kara-tippetts-heroic-cancer-fight-retold-in-new-film

Sometimes the last life-saving attempt at chemotherapy or surgery is the cause of death. What may keep you alive can also still be killing you. For those who are concerned about "playing God," would the most logically consistent thing to do be abstaining from medical treatment altogether? Where do sincere believers draw their lines between what is right and wrong, holy or unholy? Who gets to decide what sort of pain is useful for emotional and spiritual growth, and what is not?

As far as my family is concerned, there came a point in caring for Dad when we all admitted, guiltily, that we wanted this to just end already. We all were suffering, and we wanted it to be over.

One night, Dad forgot to take one of his pain pills at the prescribed time. He described his bodily sensations later as something so astronomically excruciating, he couldn't think or speak; he essentially lost his mind. How is that sort of agony even remotely redemptive? What, exactly, did Jesus mean when he promised "abundant life"?

Friends visiting his hospice bedside did their best to be encouraging. They called him "brave" and "strong." I appreciate the sentiment—perhaps my grief made me more prickly and analytical than usual—but I can think of a million other things that made my father the brave, strong man that he was. None of which have anything to do with cancer. He was brave before the diagnosis, in speaking his mind when he knew it would draw criticism; in being open and proud of his Jewishness, albeit in a nonreligious way, in a town where anyone not Christian could be looked at with suspicion.

When it comes to fighting cancer, you do what you have to do. You show up for chemotherapy. You endure the vomiting, the hair and weight loss, and burns from radiation because you have no other choice. You may do it while complaining the entire time, decrying life's unfairness, and who could judge you for that? I wouldn't consider you any less dignified than someone who bears their treatments quietly with saint-like piety.

Dad fought his way to the grave kicking and screaming, not because he feared death so much as he *loved life*. He wanted to avoid pain that would take away his ability to live with all the strength he had left; to be fully present for every hug from his kids, every kiss from my mom, every scratch of his dogs' ears, and every drop of his favorite beer.

I'm just not convinced that seeking to avoid pain at all costs is a sign of cowardice or weakness, as critics of euthanasia would suggest.

I hope you have learned at this point that whenever I ask hard questions, I rarely have the answers, and that's especially true in this case. This is one of those subjects that is best dealt with using compassion over concrete logic, and has more shades of nuance than can be summed up in any Bible verse. I have not the foggiest clue whether assisted suicide for the terminally ill is morally right or morally wrong, and I have even less of a clue as to what I would choose if I ever find myself in Brittany's or Dad's situation.

The best advice, the only advice, that I feel qualified to give is to take the situation to God; to not shut him out when making those impossible choices. Then sit quietly and listen.

Sometimes that's all we can do.

AND WE KNOW THAT ALL
THINGS WORK TOGETHER
FOR GOOD TO THOSE WHO LOVE
GOD, TO THOSE WHO ARE THE
CALLED ACCORDING TO HIS
PURPOSE.

ROMANS 8:28

Remembering RHE

In the early hours of Saturday, May 4, 2019, my phone vibrated on the nightstand next to my bed with a text from my friend Hannah. "Have you heard the latest update on Rachel?" it read, referring to one of our favorite Christian authors and bloggers, Rachel Held Evans, who had been hospitalized on Easter weekend for an allergic reaction to medication for an infection.

"Last I heard, she was being weaned out of the medically-induced coma," I wrote back.

"You need to check her website," Hannah replied. But I knew before I finished reading that sentence: Rachel had died early that morning, at the age of thirty-seven—leaving behind a devastated husband and two small children, the youngest of which was weeks away from her first birthday.

"I know her from the Internet" used to be something people said to be tongue in cheek, as in, *I don't really know
her at all*. While social media communication is certainly
no substitute for in-person relationships, the dynamic of
"internet friendships" has permanently changed what it
means to know someone "in real life." For many of us, but
especially those of us who make a living from our words,
the Internet *is* "real life." We form relationships with readers, which builds up a platform, which helps sell books
and drive website traffic. It's good, strategic marketing,
but it doesn't have to be just that.

For Rachel, you could tell that her online interactions,
mainly via Twitter, were definitely more than fame-
seeking. I'm sure her close friends and family can vouch
for this: she'd have rather used her notoriety for the ad-
vancement of God's kingdom on earth than for personal
accolades. I didn't know her personally, but when I sent
her a tweet asking about writing for a niche audience in the
Christian publishing world, she was quick to respond with
advice. I remember how it made my day when she followed me back on Twitter, and even retweeted one of my
blog posts.

She didn't just help me out as I struggled to find my
footing as a fledgling Christian writer; her willingness to
lay bare every faith-related doubt that I was too afraid to
bring up in Bible Study is what really earned her my admi-
ration. Her book *Searching for Sunday* in particular was a
lifeline to me after I dropped out of seminary with my faith
running on fumes. And when certain Christian acquaintances lectured me about how I needed to make sure my
dad accepted Jesus as his savior before the cancer took
him, Rachel's words helped give me permission to feel

anger: both at them, and at God for allowing what seemed like a very corrupt cosmic system.

Rachel didn't provide any answers to those doubts and questions, but I don't think she intended to. Rather, hers was a community of people just looking to feel validated for being imperfect, human believers.

Additionally, I was struck by just how generous and humble she was when virtually sparring with Christians who challenged her beliefs on everything from gay marriage to abortion to substitutionary atonement. She never resorted to insults or pettiness. She'd even apologize if she came across as overly harsh, or if she was in any way wrong about something. That kind of humility in a public figure, Christian or not, is rare gold these days.

Finally, the openness of her spiritual journey helped enable me to give the Episcopal Church a chance when I considered turning my back on church altogether. It kills me that I will never be able to personally thank her for that.

She never got to finish her fifth book. She never got to celebrate her little girl's first birthday. She won't get to see that little girl, or her little boy, grow to adulthood—and they are too young to have any solid memories of their mother. Her husband is now a widowed single father. It's all just so heartbreaking and cruel.

On Facebook, one of my pastor friends updated his status to simply say, "WTF, God?" That encapsulates my feelings perfectly, even though a part of me can't help remembering that Rachel's untimely death is just one of billions that have occurred throughout history. Why would I doubt God's goodness and be angry with him *now*, when these tragedies happen every day?

It's always difficult to swallow my own logic when tragedy affects me personally.

"I can't make sense of this, either," wrote one of my friends from seminary in a private Facebook message. "The only thing that makes sense is that her message had to be heard. It had to be! I can be angry, but she's not suffering right now. She's probably the happiest she's ever been. And more people will read her work now."

I replied back, "All I have to do to be angry at God is imagine her motherless children and devastated husband." Couldn't God have advanced her platform and put her books in the hands of those who need them *without* letting her die?

My friend responded, "I know—that's heartbreaking. But I also know that God takes away what the enemy intends for evil and brings good out of it somehow. She may change the face of Christianity forever, for the better, while the enemy was trying to take her out so she wouldn't."

Having known this friend for years, I know she wasn't dishing out platitudes that you hear so often in circumstances like these. She didn't say anything that isn't part of Orthodox Christian theology. Perhaps one day, I can get to a place where I believe that. I want to believe that. And yet, and yet, and yet… it's all so horribly unfair. I never actually met her, yet my heart still tightens every time I come across a tribute to her legacy. I cried all weekend long when I heard the news, and tear up still, thinking about the much-needed voice that the world just lost. Meanwhile, people like Donald Trump live into ripe old age. What was God thinking?

I can understand why some people find it easier to believe that none of this is actually real: that there is no God, no supernatural purpose behind everything that happens, no real purpose to life beyond eating, sleeping, reproducing, and dying for the next generation to do it over again until the next asteroid or global warming wipes us all out. It's almost more comforting to believe that than believe in a God who is powerful enough to save someone from an *allergic reaction*, but for some reason, opted not to.

But it wasn't fair what happened to Jesus, either, for an innocent man to be so brutally killed the way he was. I have to go back and preach to myself this basic fact, that suffering—even, from our perspective, unjust suffering—is part of this whole package we call faith. We don't have the perspective that God has. From our place backstage, we only see slivers of the action from behind the stage curtain.

It helps, too, to remember that Rachel probably wouldn't want her untimely death to turn people away from God. Rather, I believe she'd want the opposite: to draw more people nearer to him, because sacred mystery is part of the overall beauty of the Christian faith.

THERE MAY BE PAIN IN THE NIGHT, BUT JOY COMES IN THE MORNING.

Psalm 30:5

Finding Hope and Redemption in the Eucharist

I should probably hand over my Protestant membership card (assuming I ever had one) for how much thought I've given to the Eucharist lately. Just how essential is it to Christian worship? Is it the literal body and blood of Christ, or purely symbolic? And how macabre is it to eat and drink of the flesh and blood of a dead man?

A few years ago, I would have been solidly in the "purely symbolic" camp. I can't say my mind has been officially changed since joining the Episcopal Church, but now I can say this: I think there is a good deal of sacred mystery involved. Maybe I don't need to know if it's "real" or "not real." Lose the mystery, lose the wonder.

It also helps to know that the Episcopal Church does not come down heavily in favor of either side.

Regardless of what you believe about the Eucharist (or communion or whatever your tradition calls it), you begin with the same substance every time: bread.

If there's one thing that links Judaism and Christianity together in history, it is the importance that is given to bread. Manna, or bread from heaven, sustained the Jews as they wandered in the wilderness for forty years. Matzoh, or unleavened bread, is both a symbol and an ingredient included in the Passover meal, as it reminds us of the haste in which the Jews fled to escape slavery under Pharaoh.

These are no empty calories or carbs, however. Baked within the dough is the power of memory. We knead the dough and reflect back on how terrified and hurried our spiritual ancestors were as they prepared to escape their enslavement, knowing they couldn't take everything— only that which was very important. We set it to rise and consider the desperation of wandering aimlessly in the desert, with no concept of time, let alone direction, nor means of procuring food for hundreds of empty stomachs. We can smell the aroma as it bakes and rejoice at the relief and joy that comes with hope fulfilled, as God rained down that life-sustaining sustenance from the sky.

These are the stories that shape us. This is what we should think about in times of stress and trouble.

Perhaps the most important aspect of the Eucharist for me is the part of remembrance. "Do this is in remembrance of me," Jesus said, the night before he was killed. My friend Helena, who is also a Jewish-born Episcopalian, calls it a type of *yahrzeit*—the Yiddish word that refers to a death anniversary. When a death anniversary of a loved one rolls around, Jews light a special candle made for this purpose (appropriately called a *yahrzeit* candle) and recite the mourner's prayer. In the Episcopal Church, and other liturgical churches, we essentially carry out the same ritual with the bread and the wine. The two traditions may look different on the outside, but both are rooted in remembrance of past suffering.

What good does remembering do? It's more than possible to do this casually, but we really shouldn't. There's a reason that "Never Forget" is so frequently said on Holocaust Remembrance Day. Remembering the mistakes of our past is the best way to ensure that we don't repeat them today.

But we don't just remember the atrocities, the horrors, and the cruelty. We remember the people who were victimized by hatred, whether they were our great grandmothers, cousins, or other extended relatives. At any rate, they could very easily have been done to us, if we had been born in a different era, a different country, and under different circumstances. No one is ever truly "safe" because of their race, nationality, gender, or creed. The common denominator in all of us, and all of us who will ever live, is our humanity and ability to experience pain and death. At some point, we all will end up in the grave.

So, partaking of the Eucharist today, and participating in the Passover Seders of my youth, aren't just rituals for the sake of fulfilling an obligation. Pausing to remember and ritualistically partake in the suffering of Jesus, specifically, is an activity that shapes my whole week. "Do this in remembrance of me" starts with a simple command: "Do this." Why is it that I do anything? *How* am I able to do anything at all? Because of the power of the Holy Spirit in me.

That small act of remembrance shapes how I live; it enables me to pause and think twice any time I am tempted to compromise my integrity, or fire back a snarky response to some troll on Twitter.

That act of remembrance takes me back to the story of Mary Magdalene, a woman whose character and reputation have been maligned both in her culture and still today in ours. When Jesus appeared to her as his resurrected self, he dignified her by speaking her name, and trusted her to share the news of his return with the rest of the disciples in an era when female testimony was all but worthless. Whoever Mary was before, she had to be a different woman from that moment onward, because one does not experience hope so profound in the midst of grief so deep and remain unchanged.

That act of remembrance compels me to take another look at the Sermon on the Mount, where Jesus said, "Blessed are the meek" and "Blessed are those who mourn," because there is more to be read between the lines.

Jesus also says, blessed are the parents whose children are no longer with them, either in the grave or on the other side of the border.

Jesus also says, blessed are the couples whose hearts are full of hope, but whose wombs remain empty.

Blessed are those who hide bruises inflicted by the people who are supposed to love them; or who hide the wounds they inflict upon themselves.

Blessed are those who are told by people with Live Laugh Love signs in their homes to just smile and be happy, go outside, or try doing yoga—anything but prescription medicine for their unseen pain.

Blessed are those who hurt too much to get out of bed or perform even the simplest acts of self-care.

Blessed are those who are trapped in the throes of addiction, whose bodies cannot function without poison.

Blessed are those who are still not "over it", who know in their hearts that grief fundamentally changes a person, and they will never truly "get over it."

Blessed are the ones who remain in the closet, certain that revealing their true selves will cost them everything.

Blessed are those who are still trying to adjust to their "new normal," if they've even figured out what that looks like.

The Eucharist is not "just bread"; it's hope and redemption all baked into one.

I HAVE TOLD YOU THESE THINGS,
SO THAT IN ME YOU MAY HAVE
PEACE. IN THIS WORLD YOU
WILL HAVE TROUBLE.
BUT TAKE HEART!
I HAVE OVERCOME THE WORLD.

JOHN 16:33

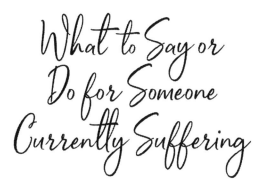

What to Say or Do for Someone Currently Suffering

I recognize the impossibility of giving universal instructions to friends and well-meaning acquaintances of sufferers when everyone's experience is different. What is helpful to one person may be irritating or offensive to another. But speaking from my own experiences, here are some of the things that were most beneficial to me during some of the hardest, most painful moments of my life:

"How can I help?"

There are some times when everyone just knows that nothing will be okay, at least not any time soon. So rather than trying to come up with the right words when they may not exist, I recommend focusing on tasks that the sufferer may not have time or energy for. My family had neighbors who worked in shifts to walk our dogs during long hours of chemotherapy, mow our lawn, bring us meals, and run other household-related errands that otherwise would have been left undone.

It's possible that the person suffering may not even be aware of what they need, so feel free to suggest something. Ask if you can bring dinner over. Offer to take her kids to the park or the library for a bit. Shovel their driveway in the winter. These things won't reverse or undo a tragedy, obviously, but it is so much easier to bear grief in community than alone.

"I'm so sorry you're going through this."

Again, when no words are capable of taking away someone's pain, acknowledging it can make a huge difference. Provide ample space for anger, sadness, despair, and other raw, naked emotions that may be locked away inside. Be a sounding board rather than an armchair therapist. Offer a hug, a tissue, or a warm beverage as your friend grieves. Let him or her know that it's okay to simply feel.

Check in regularly.

This one can be tricky, because some people resent being asked, "How are you?" after their world just fell apart; especially when everyone knows that they are not "fine." On the other hand, others may appreciate being asked about their wellbeing. You know your friend or relative best. You don't have to lead with "How are you?" but instead, "Just checking in," or "I haven't forgotten about you" or "I'm thinking of you."

My annual text message to my friend K on the anniversary of her brother's suicide is usually, "How's it going?" At this point in our friendship, we understand the real message behind the words. Come up with your own ritualistic "checking in" message to let your loved one know you haven't forgotten them. One of the worst things you can do to a good friend in a crisis is back away from them until it all blows over. They will likely feel abandoned by you.

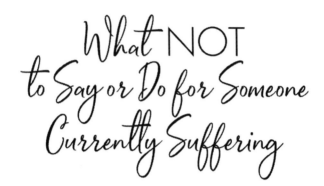

What NOT to Say or Do for Someone Currently Suffering

A dmittedly, this list is a bit longer than the previous list of do's. I guess that's because knowing the right thing to say or do is harder. It's a lot easier to be insensitive or callous to people in pain, even if that's not your intent.

Just as with the previous list, everyone's response to crisis will be different. The things that I find offensive or unhelpful may be life-giving for others. Use discernment and discretion.

With that caveat out of the way, here are a few things I recommend *not* saying or doing when someone you know is suffering:

"Everything happens for a reason."

Unless you're able to provide that reason, I recommend burying this statement forever (and even if you did know the reason, chances are that the sufferer doesn't want to hear it). This is trivializing at best, and cruel at worst. It has potential to drive people away from God; though a god that uses illness or death as a means to punish sin or simply because he "needs another angel" isn't one who is worthy of worship.

Putting time limits on grief

In Judaism, there is a seven-day mourning period in which the close relatives of the deceased are taken care of by their communities. They don't engage in any cooking, cleaning, or chores; they don't wear makeup, put on shoes, or leave their homes. Only when the seven-day period is over do they begin the arduous process of returning to the rhythm of their ordinary lives.

But that's not to say that the grieving ends after that designated mourning period. Grief can be felt for weeks, months, or years after a loss, especially if it's one that upends someone's entire way of life. Don't expect the grieving person to "bounce back" any time soon. Some losses can permanently change a person. Expecting them to ever "get over it" is not only egregiously insensitive, but also ignorant as to how grief even works. Just don't say or expect it.

Sharing your own miracle story

This is a deeply personal one for me. I understand that people meant it as encouragement when they told me how God miraculously healed them of the exact same condition that killed my father. But rather than restoring my faith, these stories created false hope. Not every illness has a cure. Not every person will be healed. This is a fact of life, not an indictment of God's faithfulness. Still, these stories strike a wounded place in my heart that make me wonder if God loves some of his children more than others. Why was Susie's cancer more worthy of healing than my dad's? Was he only a few prayers short of being granted full remission?

If your hurting friend is a Christian, perhaps it will be helpful to remind them that God sees their pain and is sitting with them through it. But don't make promises on his behalf; you don't know what is going to happen.

"I know how you feel."

Even if you've experienced the exact same loss, you haven't experienced it the exact same way. You are a different person, with different circumstances and experiences that have informed your responses. So no, you don't know exactly how someone else feels, nor can you.

"At least…"

"At least you are young and can get pregnant again."

"At least he didn't hurt you worse."

"At least she had a good life."

The words "at least" are the great minimizer. Even with the best of intentions, their impact is to trivialize. I propose that any sentence starting with those two words in response to a grieving or suffering person should just never be uttered, ever.

Books to Help You Through Dark Nights of the Soul

I tried to include a variety of different perspectives, depending on your faith tradition and circumstances for suffering:

The Radiant Midnight by Melissa Maimone

Man's Search for Meaning by Viktor Frankl

The Problem of Pain by C.S. Lewis

Lord Willing? by Jessica Kelley

Seeking Peace by Johann Christoph Arnold

Rare Bird by Anna Whiston-Donaldson

Glorious Weakness by Alia Joy

Good God, Lousy World, and Me by Holly Burkhalter

... and Life Comes Back by Tricia Lott Williford

Soul Bare, an anthology edited by Cara Sexton

More Than You Can Handle by Nate Pyle

Confessions of a Funeral Director by Caleb Wilde

When Breath Becomes Air by Paul Kalanithi

Modern Loss by Rebecca Soffer and Gabrielle Birkner

The Still Point of the Turning World by Emily Rapp

Everything Happens for a Reason (and Other Lies I've Loved) by Kate Bowler

Walking with God Through Pain and Suffering by Timothy Keller

Music to Help You Through Dark Nights of the Soul

A mix of Christian and secular:

Gravity Happens by Kate Voegele

Nothing is Wasted by Jason Gray

Always There by Dan Nichols and Eighteen

Changing World by Kutless

Armor by Sara Bareilles

For the Moments I Feel Faint by Relient K

Singing in the Rain by Simple Plan

Fighter by Christina Aguilera

When I Look to the Sky by Train

Shake it Out by Florence and the Machine

Face of Grace by Anna Gilbert

Invincible by Kelly Clarkson

We're Not Gonna Take It by Twisted Sister

These Old Wings by Anna Nalick

Wounded Healer by Audrey Assad

It Is Well with My Soul—any version of your choosing.

Dear Reader,

If this book impacted you in some way, I would greatly appreciate it if you took the time to write a brief review (like only a sentence or two) on Amazon or Goodreads. Your feedback not only helps potential new readers, but also makes an impact on the Great and Powerful Internet Algorithms so that people are more likely to find this book when using relevant search terms.

To stay up to date with my writing projects, blog posts, and book recommendations, please subscribe to my newsletter: https://bit.ly/2TrYYkk

– Sb

Acknowledgments

A huge thank you to my team of beta readers: Laura Johnson, Kristen Hruby, Hannah Jackson, and Allison Kennedy. The best friends are the ones who have full permission to be blunt and honest, and I am grateful that you are those people in my life.

To Joshua, who has endured dating and marriage to a woman who has written about rape culture, mental illness, and now suffering. "A lot" (always).

To JC Wing, my editor; Amy Queau, my talented cover designer; and Julie Titus, my formatter. My books would not be possible without you.

To the folks at Mac Shack, who were able to restore this manuscript when my laptop crashed, and I thought it was gone forever. Thank you for reminding me to back up my content regularly, which I obviously did not do before. You are true heroes.

To my followers on social media who helped fund this book through Patreon, shared pre-order links on their platforms, and rally behind me always. Your support means the world to me.

Finally, to all the Christians who said, "That sucks" and offered to bring food, walk the dogs, and run the errands when shit hit the fan, and never tried to smooth over my pain with platitudes that belong on refrigerator magnets. Keep on doing the Lord's work.

Other Titles by Sarahbeth Caplin

Confessions of a Prodigal Daughter: a memoir

Where There's Smoke: a novella

Public Displays of Convention: a novel
(available as an eBook only)

A Stunning Accusation: a novel

Sorting Myself: a collection of poetry
(available in paperback only)

Things You Can't Un-see: essays

REFERENCE NOTES

1 "Kim Davis." *Wikipedia*, Wikimedia Foundation, 19 May 2019, en.wikipedia.org/wiki/Kim_Davis

2 Quillin, Martha. "Baptist Leader Paige Patterson Stands by His Controversial Advice to Spousal Abuse Victims." *Newsobserver*, Raleigh News & Observer, 1 May 2018, www.newsobserver.com/news/local/article210215494.html

3 Chumley, Cheryl K. "God-given, Not Government Granted, Guides 2nd Amendment." *The Washington Times*, The Washington Times, 29 May 2018, www.washingtontimes.com/news/2018/may/29/god-given-not-government-granted-guides-second-ame/

4 Moore, Russell. "What a Stupid Bumper Sticker Can Tell Us About American Christianity." *ChurchLeaders*, 26 Apr. 2019, https://churchleaders.com/pastors/pastor-articles/314862-stupid-bumper-sticker-can-tell-us-american-christianity.html

5 "Dave Ramsey's 7 Baby Steps." *Dave Ramsey's 7 Baby Steps | DaveRamsey.com*, www.daveramsey.com/dave-ramsey-7-baby-steps#baby_step_1

6 Spencer, John, and John Spencer. "Five Reasons the 'Walk Up, Not Out' Meme Is So Problematic." *Medium,* Medium, 15 Mar. 2018, https://link.medium.com/QwmClD9ReZ

7 "Slideshow: Pictures of Celebrities With Depression." *WebMD*, WebMD, www.webmd.com/depression/ss/slideshow-depression-celebs

8 "A Little Weird? Prone to Depression? Blame Your Creative Brain." *Psychology Today*, Sussex Publishers, www.psychologytoday.com/us/blog/prescriptions-life/201204/little-weird-prone-depression-blame-your-creative-brain

9 "Brittany Maynard." *Wikipedia*, Wikimedia Foundation, 1 May 2019, en.wikipedia.org/wiki/Brittany_Maynard

10 Jessup, John. "'God Is Present in Pain:' Kara Tippetts' Heroic Cancer Fight Retold in New Film." *CBN News*, 21 Mar. 2019, https://www1.cbn.com/cbnnews/us/2019/march/god-is-present-in-pain-kara-tippetts-heroic-cancer-fight-retold-in-new-film.